Young
Devotions for^ Disciples

The Basics

Matthew J. Cochran

Devotions for Young Disciples: The Basics

ISBN-13: 978-0-9849983-4-0

ISBN-10: 0984998349

DEDICATION

This book is dedicated to the children of KidCity at Christ Fellowship of Tampa and to their parents, our partners in ministry. I love you guys.

INTRODUCTION

Though I've written devotions for many years and have published several books of devotions, this is my first attempt at writing specifically to children. Having made a ministry move to working with kids from kindergarten through 5th grade, I thought it was only right that I took my mission of making disciples with me to the new venture. I have a heart for kids and I have a deep desire to see them come to know Jesus in a personal way.

I'm known for my criticisms of children's ministry curriculum because I feel that much of it can be fluff and it stops short of telling the whole story of God's redemption and Christ's work on the cross. It seems that we often have to un-teach people what we taught them as children in order for them to have a healthy understanding of Christian doctrine. But if we just teach them correctly the first time, we don't have to repair the damage later on.

Parents, I want this to be a tool for you to use in helping your kids to understand the basics of the Christian faith; who God is, what the Bible is, who we are created to be, what sin is, and what Jesus has done about it. This is a starting point. Talk to your kids about the Scriptures and memorize the verses along with them. You won't ever regret having done it.

This book of devotions is intended for children between the ages of 8 and 12, but you know your own child's maturity level, so you make the call on whether it's appropriate for them.

I'd love to hear your feedback or receive your questions concerning what's in this book (or not in it). You can email me at matt@christfellowshiptampa.com.

To see more children's devotions like this, visit www.kiddevotions.com.

1 WHO IS GOD?

Have you ever wondered who God is? Sometimes you sit and listen in church about all of this stuff in the Bible and all of these stories about people who lived a long time ago and you just think, "I wish I knew who God really is."

It can be a hard thing to understand who God is. We refer to the "nature and character" of God or the "attributes" of God, but that doesn't make much sense to kids. What that means is just that there are certain things that describe God that don't describe anyone else.

For instance, no one has every made something out of nothing except for God. Before Him, there was nothing and yet He made the earth, the skies and waters, the animals, the stars and other planets, and even people. If you made something, it would have to be made out of something else. Only God can make something out of nothing.

So who is God? Well, that can't be answered all in one day, so we'll take a few to look at some of the things you might want to know about Him. For today, just know that God is the Creator of all things. You were created by God just like the earth, Adam & Eve, your parents, and trees.

Read Genesis 1:1-31 in your Bible to find out more about creation.

Let's work on memorizing Genesis 1:1 this week:

"In the beginning, God created the heavens and the earth."

2 GOD KNOWS EVERYTHING

You've probably heard the story of Adam and Eve (If you haven't, read Genesis 2-3 in your Bible). God created Adam and allowed him to rule over all of the animals of the earth and name them. It wasn't good enough, though, for Adam to be alone. God wanted Adam to have a friend, so He created the woman, Eve.

God let Adam and Eve do pretty much whatever they wanted to do in the garden where they lived, but He did give them one rule. He told them they could eat from any tree except for one. Do you remember what happened next? Yep. They ate from that one tree. The one they weren't supposed to eat from. And then what did they do? They hid from God.

Have you ever done something like this? Did you ever do something you knew was wrong and then hide from your parents? They may or may not have known what you did, but God definitely knew, just like He knew what Adam and Eve had done. They couldn't hid from God because He knows everything!

Some people think this is a bad thing because God knows all of the wrong things that you do, but actually it's a good thing because God knows you better than anyone and

He loves you anyway. He loves you a ton. We'll talk more about that tomorrow though.

Even if you've read about Adam and Eve before, look at Genesis 2-3 and think about how God already knew what Adam and Eve were doing before they admitted it.

Let's keep working on memorizing Genesis 1:1:

"In the beginning, God created the heavens and the earth."

Find someone to practice with!

3 GOD LOVES YOU

Sometimes we all do things that aren't what God would want us to do. That's called sin. Have you ever sinned? The bad news is, we've all sinned. The Bible even says so in Romans 3:23. Sometimes we don't tell the truth, or maybe we disobey something we were told to do, whatever the sin is, we all do it.

So how can God still love us if we disobey Him? The Bible says that He wants us to be perfect (Leviticus 20:26), but we can't be because of our sin. We're unable to please Him if we can't be totally sinless and we just can't do that. But there's good news!

God loves you. In fact, He loves all of His creation. In John 3:16, He says that He sent His Son, Jesus, to take our punishment for the bad things we've done. He did that because He loves us. Do you love people that treat you badly? It's hard isn't it? We don't like to keep caring for people who don't care for us, but God loves each of us even though we treat Him badly by sinning.

If you understand this one thing, you'll know a lot about God. When He sent Jesus, it wasn't only to pay for your sins. Jesus also gave you His perfection if you believe in Him. Remember, you need to be perfect in order to please

God, but you can't do it on your own. Jesus is perfect *for* you! That means if you believe in Him, you can be God's friend! The Bible even says that means God adopts you as His own child (John 1:12)!

Read Psalm 118:1-4. How long does God's love last?

Let's review Genesis 1:1 one more time. Do you have it memorized yet?

"In the beginning, God created the heavens and the earth."

4 GOD IS PERFECT

Yesterday we talked about how God is perfect and He wants us to be perfect. Since we can't do that on our own, He sent Jesus.

So why is it important that God is perfect? Well, first of all, because you're not. I'm not either. We make mistakes, we mess up. God never makes a mistake. Not one. Ever. God not only *doesn't* make mistakes, He *can't* make mistakes.

That's good news for those of us who trust in Him! When we pray, we know that we're asking God, the one who doesn't make any mistakes. When we think He didn't answer our prayers the right way, we know that can't be true because He's perfect. He always does what He means to do and He never messes it up. We can really trust Him!

God has a plan for your life. And since He's perfect, you know it's a good plan! Even when things don't seem like they're going right, you can know that it's going to work out the way God planned it.

Joseph was someone who had to trust God through a lot of bad stuff happening. Read about his life in Genesis 37-45. Do you think Joseph ever doubted God?

Memorize John 3:16.

"For God so loved the world, that he gave his only Son, that whoever believes in him should not perish but have eternal life."

Get some help if you need it!

5 GOD IS GOOD

God is good, all the time. It's important that we know this, because just remembering that God knows everything might make us scared that He'll punish us. Just remembering that He created everything and that He's really powerful might make us worry about what He'll do. But if we remember that He loves us and that He's good, we'll never have to worry.

Even though God has all of the power in the world, He doesn't ever try to just hurt you for no reason. He doesn't ever try to make you afraid or take things away from you just because He feels like it. God is good so we know if He plans for something to happen in our lives it must be for good. There are a lot of examples in the Bible of people who had to go through some rough times but found out that it was for God's good plans. Can you name a person like that from the Bible?

Read Romans 8:28 to find out something God said about His plans for you.

Do you have John 3:16 memorized yet? Practice for one more day:

"For God so loved the world, that he gave his only Son, that whoever believes in him should not perish but have eternal life."

6 WHO IS JESUS?

You've probably heard some stories about Jesus. You know the things He did like heal sick people, make the blind see again, and even die on the cross. But do you really understand who Jesus is? He wasn't just a man who lived on the earth for a while. He was much more than that!

Over the next few days, we'll look at some things that help us to better understand Jesus, starting with the fact that Jesus is God. There are way too many things about Jesus to talk about in only one week, but we'll focus on some of the most important ones and then at the end there will be a list for you to look at to discover even more.

Jesus is the most important person who ever lived and what you know about who He is is the most important thing about your life. Did you know that Jesus is that big a deal? What you think about Jesus really is the thing that determines your future more than anything else.

Read about when Jesus was born as a baby in Luke 2:1-7. What's special about the way Jesus was born?

How are you doing at memorizing Bible verses? Today, take a look at John 1:1 and start trying to memorize it:

"In the beginning was the Word, and the Word was with God, and the Word was God."

7 JESUS IS GOD

Sometime when people hear that Jesus is God, they think, "But I thought Jesus was the SON of God!" It is true that Jesus is the Son of God, but it's not a son like parents have here on earth. Jesus wasn't born, He has always been, even before the beginning of time. The Bible says He was in the beginning with God and He was God (John 1:1).

So how can He be both the Son of God and God himself? Well, there's a really hard to explain part of who God is, called the Trinity. God is the Father, the Son, and the Holy Spirit. They're all God, but it doesn't mean that there are three Gods. See what I mean by hard to explain? For now, all you need to understand is that Jesus is no less than God the Father, who is usually who we think of when we say "God."

There are lots of places in the Bible that talk about Jesus being God and even Jesus said that He is God. Look at Colossians 1:16 and 1:19 to see how it was Jesus that was used in creating the world and that He is God in a body. Now look back at the story of creation in Genesis 1:1 and think about it knowing that Jesus was creating.

Keep practicing memorization of John 1:1 today:

"In the beginning was the Word, and the Word was with God, and the Word was God."

8 JESUS IS SAVIOR

One of the most important things you could ever know in your life is who Jesus is. I'm sure you probably have heard in church or from someone else that Jesus died on the cross, but do you know why? Do you know what His dying on the cross did for you? If you do know, that's awesome! If you don't, you need to know.

First you need to know why Jesus had to die. You see, we're all sinners, that means we disobey God. He wants us to be perfect, just like He is, but none of us can do it. The Bible calls this falling short of God's glory (Romans 3:23). Only someone who's perfect can be in heaven with God, so none of us can make it... unless...

The good news is that Jesus was perfect, the only perfect person who ever lived, because He is God himself who became a man. Because He was sinless while He lived on earth, He was the perfect sacrifice for our sins. The Bible says in Romans 6:23 that the price that must be paid for our sin is death. But since Jesus chose to die in our place, He paid that price! This is why we call Him our Savior, because He saved us. If it weren't for Him, we couldn't be with God.

If we trust in Jesus and ask God to forgive us for all of the times we've disobeyed Him, He'll save us and help us to live for Him. Isn't that great? You know what's even better? Jesus didn't stay dead. He's alive! We'll talk more about that tomorrow, though.

Do you have John 1:1 memorized? Let's work on Acts 4:12 now. This one will take longer to learn: "

And there is salvation in no one else, for there is no other name under heaven given among men by which we must be saved."

9 JESUS IS ALIVE

It can be sad to think about how Jesus had to die because we've disobeyed God, but we shouldn't stay sad because Jesus didn't stay dead. He's alive! When we celebrate on Easter, we're celebrating that Jesus came back to life by the power of God and later He went back into heaven.

After He came back to life, Jesus went to visit all of His friends, the disciples, to show them that He was alive. Some of them believed Him right away, but others wanted to see proof that He was really Jesus. He showed them on His hands where the nails had gone through to hold Him onto the cross. He even ate with them to show that He was real. Before Jesus went back up to heaven, He had a message for His disciples and for me and you.

He said that He would always be with us, even though He left to go back to heaven. Do you know how it is that Jesus is always with us? Read John 16:7 to see how Jesus promised a Helper, the Holy Spirit, to all who trust in Him. While Jesus sits in heaven with God, allowing us to be able to pray (Ephesians 2:18), the Holy Spirit is in us, helping us to pray, to obey God, to understand the Bible, and even helping us to worship God.

Jesus is very much alive! Read John 21:1-14 to see some things Jesus did after He was raised from the dead.

Keep studying and memorizing Acts 4:12:

"And there is salvation in no one else, for there is no other name under heaven given among men by which we must be saved."

10 JESUS IS COMING BACK

Not only is Jesus alive right now in heaven, He's promised that He'll come back to us. When He does return, it will be to bring all of His followers to be part of heaven. He even said there will be new earth (Revelation 21:1)!

It's important that we know that Jesus is coming back for a couple of reasons. First, because it gives us a great hope. If we know that Jesus is returning we know that everything will work out for us in the end. Second, knowing that He's coming back helps us to realize that we need to always be prepared for His return. We shouldn't just get ready for Him later, we should do it now.

The Bible talks a lot about what will happen when Jesus returns in the book of Revelation. Since it's kind of hard to understand, ask an adult to explain to you what some of those things are. It's really exciting!

Keep working on Acts 4:12. Do you have it memorized yet?

"And there is salvation in no one else, for there is no other name under heaven given among men by which we must be saved."

11 WHO IS THE HOLY SPIRIT?

Some stuff in the Bible is hard to understand. Actually, there's a lot of things about God that are hard to understand. How can God be everywhere at one time? How did He create everything by speaking? Stuff like that. Probably one of the things about God that's most misunderstood is the fact that He's the Father, the Son, and the Holy Spirit all at once. And while most people seem to understand who God the Father is, and Jesus the Son, they're not sure what to think about the Holy Spirit.

Have you ever heard someone call the Holy Spirit the "Holy Ghost?" That can be pretty confusing because it makes you think the Holy Spirit is some kind of weird invisible ghost thing. In fact, the Spirit isn't a thing. He's God. We'll talk more about that tomorrow.

Ghosts are scary, but God care about all of His people and He's got good plans for you. His Holy Spirit is sent to help you, to make you feel better, to make you brave, and to help other people through you. There won't be time to cover every little topic about the Holy Spirit that we could possibly talk about, but we'll try to take a good look at just who He is and what He means to you.

Let's memorize a Bible verse about the Holy Spirit. In John 14:16, Jesus says,

"And I will ask the Father, and he will give you another Helper, to be with you forever"

12 THE HOLY SPIRIT IS NOT AN "IT"

When you think of the Holy Spirit, what do you think of? Maybe you've never even heard that name before. Maybe in your church they say the Holy Ghost. Lots of people have different thoughts about the Holy Spirit. The most important thing is what God said in the Bible.

The Holy Spirit is mentioned all throughout the Bible, both in the times before Jesus came to live on earth (the Old Testament) and after He came (the New Testament). The Holy Spirit guided the people of the Old Testament just like He does for us today, but Jesus spoke about Him in a new way. He said that the Holy Spirit would be sent after He went back to heaven. In other words, when Jesus returned to heaven, the Spirit took His place on earth.

Why do I say that the Holy Spirit is not an "it?" Because things don't think for themselves or do things on their own. People do. God does. And the Holy Spirit is God. He has a purpose and He speaks to you. He spoke to the men who wrote the Bible to tell them what to say, He helped create the world, He helps you to pray, and He cares about you.

Let's keep memorizing that same
Bible verse. John 14:16:

"And I will ask the Father, and he will
give you another Helper, to be with
you forever"

13 THE HOLY SPIRIT IS OUR HELPER

When Jesus rose from the dead after dying on the cross, He spent some time with His disciples, but then He explained to them that He had to leave to go back to heaven. He told them not to worry, though, because a helper would come for them. Since He couldn't be with them, or us, on the earth anymore, He sent the Holy Spirit to help us.

It's cool to think about what it would have been liked to walk with Jesus while He was here, but He actually said that it's even better to have the Holy Spirit than to have Him here with us (John 16:7). Jesus could only be in one place at a time, but the Holy Spirit can be all places, He can even be in our hearts.

So what does He help us with? He helps us to pray because sometimes we don't even know what we should say (Romans 8:26). He helps us to know what is right and what is wrong (John 16:8). He helps us to understand God and the Bible (John 14:26). He even helps us to not be scared (We'll talk more about that tomorrow). There's a lot of ways, even more than these that I listed, that the Holy Spirit helps us. Can you think of any more ways?

Keep working on memorizing John 14:16.

"And I will ask the Father, and he will give you another Helper, to be with you forever."

Do you have it yet?

14 THE HOLY SPIRIT IS OUR COMFORTER

We all get scared sometimes. We all can get worried that something won't work out the way we want it to. But God doesn't want us to be afraid. He even sent the Holy Spirit to keep us from being afraid.

There are lots of bad things that can happen in life, but none of them are so big that God can't handle them. He's got everything under control and He wants us to trust Him. In those times that we have a hard time with that, He promises to help. He reminds us of who He is and what He's done by the Holy Spirit bringing things to our thoughts.

The Bible says that the Holy Spirit reminds us that we're children of God if we've trusted in Him to save us (See the final chapter of this book if you have questions about that). He helps us to feel better because He lets us know that He loves us. And if God loves us, what could possible keep us from being happy for very long?

Keep up the great work memorizing John 14:16.

"And I will ask the Father, and he will give you another Helper, to be with you forever"

15 THE HOLY SPIRIT IS GOD

I mentioned this before, but I want to make sure you remember. The Holy Spirit isn't just some thing or someone that God sent to help us. He IS God. The reason why He can help us is because He is God. The reason why He can comfort us is because He is God. The reason why He is powerful in our lives is because...you got it...He is God.

God is invisible, yet He showed himself when Jesus came to live on the earth (Colossians 1:15). When He went back up to heaven, we had no more way of seeing Him, but now He lives in us. If you want to read a very interesting story about the Holy Spirit, look at Acts 1:6-11 and Acts 2:1-12. The Holy Spirit did some amazing things in the lives of the disciples and He can do some amazing things in your life too!

Can you think of one thing that God is doing right now to help you, comfort you, or make you more like Him?

Do you have John 14:16 memorized yet? Let's say it one more time,

"And I will ask the Father, and he will give you another Helper, to be with you forever"

16 WHAT IS SIN?

Have you ever heard someone talk about sin and wonder what that means? Sometimes people define sin as the bad choices we make or the bad things we do. That's a good start, but sin is more than that. It started long ago, with Adam and Eve, the very first people.

You've probably heard of Adam and Eve. God created them after the earth and plants and animals and all of that. They were the first humans who ever lived and they had a perfect place and a friendship with God. They talked to God everyday and they were very close to Him. Can you imagine hanging out with God every day? They did that. But then they did something to mess it all up.

God had asked Adam and Eve not to eat the fruit from only one of the trees in the garden. You know what happened though? That's right, they ate it anyway. They sinned. That means they went against God's commandment. That's one meaning of sin.

The really bad thing is their sin meant that everyone who ever came after them would be someone who sinned too. That's called a sin nature. It means we're all born as sinners and there's nothing we can do about it. We will all sin in our lives (Romans 3:23). That part of us is another meaning of sin. And it's for that sin that Jesus had to die in our place. He had to earn back our friendship with God that Adam and Eve messed up, because we can't earn it back on our own. We'll talk more about what He did later this week.

How are things going with memorizing verses? Let's memorize this one: 1 Corinthians 15:22

"For as in Adam all die, so also in Christ shall all be made alive."

17 THE PENALTY FOR SIN

In this life we have consequences we have to face for when we do bad things or break the law. For you it might be something like being grounded from electronic devices for a certain amount of time until you apologize for something. For adults it might be getting arrested and put in jail for doing something really bad. But God has given an even bigger price to pay for our sin.

In Romans, it says that the wages (that means payment or price) of sin is death (Romans 6:23). That doesn't mean we just die instantly when we sin, it means the result of our sin is that we end up having to die and be separated from God. This is the same for everyone. No one can buy their way out of it or even do enough good things to be forgiven. Remember the verse from yesterday? Romans 3:23 says that everyone has sinned. Everyone but Jesus.

The good news is that the one person who never sinned paid the price for our sin. He did it in our place. We'll still die when our lives are over here on earth, but we'll be with God in heaven if we've trusted in Jesus, instead of separated from Him forever. Tomorrow we'll look more at what it was that Jesus did for us.

Keep memorizing 1 Corinthians 15:22

"For as in Adam all die, so also in Christ shall all be made alive."

Do you know what that means yet?

18 THE PRICE PAID FOR OUR SIN

Because of our sin, we were separated from God, unable to be His friend. We had a price to pay for being sinful and the price was death (Romans 6:23). The only way that we could get out of owing that payment for sin was if someone else died in our place. But not just anyone could do it. No, it had to be the perfect sacrifice. It had to be someone who actually had never sinned. So God made Jesus, who knew no sin, become sin in our place (2 Corinthians 5:21) so that we could be right with Him.

When Jesus died on the cross, He took on all of the sin of the world. Everything we've ever done wrong was paid for in that act. But, did you know that Jesus did more than just die for our sin? In order to be right with God, a person has to be righteous (that means we'd have to be perfect). Since we can't be perfect, even after Jesus took all of our sins (We would just commit more sins), He gave us HIS righteousness. He took our bad and gave us His good.

Now, if we trust in Jesus to forgive our sins, we become children of God! We get to be part of God's family! There's more on that in tomorrow's devotion.

Do you have 1 Corinthians 15:22 memorized yet?

"For as in Adam all die, so also in Christ shall all be made alive."

19 THE FREE GIFT

By now you know what the price to be paid for sin is: death. You also know that because Jesus lived a life without sin, He was able to take your place and pay the price for you. When He died on the cross, He took your punishment. But did you know He also gave you a gift?

In the same verse that tells us the "wages of sin is death," we learn that "the free gift of God is eternal life in Christ Jesus our Lord." (Romans 6:23) We not only don't have to face our punishment, we get to spend forever with God because of Jesus. The forgiveness that He buys from God makes it so that we can be adopted into God's family.

We don't do anything to deserve or earn this. It's all a free gift from God that Jesus made sure we could get. Doesn't that just show you how much God loves you? If you put your trust in Jesus for the forgiveness of your sins and repent (that means to turn away from your sins), He'll forgive you and bring you into His family.

Let's memorize Ephesians 2:8 the rest of this week.

"For by grace you have been saved through faith. And this is not your own doing; it is the gift of God"

20 GRACE

What is grace? Is it something you say at the dinner table before you eat? We talked yesterday about how God's forgiveness is a free gift bought and paid for by Jesus. I mentioned how we can't do anything to earn or deserve that free gift. That's part of what grace is.

When God doesn't give us what we really deserve (death, according to Romans 6:23), but He gives us something wonderful that we could never deserve (His forgiveness, adoption into His family, eternal life with Him), He is showing us grace. It's not just about forgiveness though.

You have special talents and abilities that no one else has. God gave you those when He planned out who you were going to be. You didn't do anything to make yourself have those gifts, you got them by God's grace. Maybe you have always been able to sing well. God gave you that talent. Maybe for you it's an ability to cook really good food without needing a cookbook. That talent is from God. It's His grace. Many things in this life are not earned and they come from the Giver of all good and perfect gifts, God (James 1:17).

We should thank Him. Will you pray right now and thank God for all of His grace?

Keep memorizing Ephesians 2:8.

"For by grace you have been saved through faith. And this is not your own doing; it is the gift of God"

21 WHAT IS THE BIBLE?

I'm sure you've at least seen a Bible. You might own one, or maybe at least your parents own one. Have you ever wondered what it really is? Does it seem like a rule book, full of things you're supposed to do and not supposed to do? Some people look at it that way, but it's so much more.

Some say that the Bible is God's love letter to His people, and this is also true, but again there's more to it than that. While it is full of God's love, there also are rules and laws, stories to give us an idea of how things happened in history, and even warnings about the future. There are predictions of the future that told of Jesus before He came to earth, stories of His life, and lots of things leading up to it. Actually, the whole Bible is about Jesus.

We're told that God has spoken to people in many different ways and that the most important way was through coming to earth as Jesus (Hebrews 1:1-3). But since Jesus isn't just walking around where we can see Him anymore, the best thing we have is the book about Him. The Bible is God's message to us. Everything we need to know can be found in His Word.

We're going to look at who wrote the Bible, how we can know it's true, and how to read it.

Here's a new Bible verse to memorize this week: 1 Peter 1:25

"but the word of the Lord remains forever. And this word is the good news that was preached to you."

22 GOD WROTE THE BIBLE

So who wrote the Bible? There are 66 "books" within the book we call the Bible and they were written down by lots of different authors. The real deal, though, is that God told those people what He wanted them to write. We say that the words of the Bible are "inspired" by God or "breathed out" by God (2 Timothy 3:16). HE wrote the Bible!

The Lord used to speak to people in many different ways to reveal himself. He shows us who He is through His creation (Psalm 19:1), and He showed us everything we could ever need to know about himself through Jesus (Hebrews 1:2). Since Jesus is not walking on earth anymore, God chose to speak to us through His Word, the Bible. In it, He tells us all we need to know.

We know because of the Bible who God is, what He wants us to do, what He wants us to stop doing, what He wants us to learn, and what His plans are. If we'll take the time to read it, the Bible will tell us a whole lot. When it gets hard, we can ask the author for His help in understanding.

Keep working on memorizing 1 Peter 1:25

"but the word of the Lord remains forever. And this word is the good news that was preached to you."

23 HOW CAN I KNOW THE BIBLE IS TRUE?

There are a lot of books out there and many of them say different things that don't agree with each other. It's hard to know which one is right! The same is true in religious books. Christians rely on the Bible as our way of knowing what God is like and what He expects from us. Other religions say that the Bible isn't true. How can we know that it is?

There are a few ways that people who study the Bible use to test if its correct. They look at the events and people from history mentioned in the Bible to make sure they actually happened and existed. We're also able to look at the predictions in the Bible and see that most of them have already come true. God keeps all of His promises and He cannot lie!

Another way we can know that the Bible is true is because the Bible says so. Now, some think this doesn't make sense and lots of other books would claim that they're true too. But nothing in the Bible contradicts (says the opposite of) anything else that the Bible says. It all supports itself.

2 Timothy 3:16-17 says that God authored the Bible and that we can trust it. Hebrews 4:12says that the Holy Spirit

speaks to us through the Bible. There are a ton of verses in God's Word that help to understand this more, but let's stick with these for now. Can you find any more by doing your own search?

Let's keep working on memorizing 1 Peter 1:25

"but the word of the Lord remains forever. And this word is the good news that was preached to you."

Do you have it yet?

24 ARE ALL BIBLES THE SAME?

Have you ever been listening to someone who was reading the Bible out loud, trying to follow along in your own Bible, but it seems like everything they're saying is different? You know you're in the right place, but nothing they're saying is in your Bible. That's because there are different translations of the original documents that were put together to form one Bible.

The books of the Bible were written in languages like Hebrew and Greek. Many people who study the Bible as part of their job find different meanings to words from the original languages used, so we end up with different Bibles in the English language. So who is right about the real meanings? That's a hard question to answer.

People sometimes argue about which Bible translation is correct, but they forget two things. 1) God is the author of the Bible, it says what He intends it to say. 2) God is the interpreter of the Bible within our hearts. He can help us to understand what He wants to say to us, even if a certain translation does get the meaning wrong.

All Bibles are not the same, but God always remains the same no matter how many years pass. What He wanted the people of long ago to know, He wants us to know. Our job is to ask Him to help us understand and then read with an open heart.

Here's a new verse to memorize: 2 Peter 1:20

"knowing this first of all, that no prophecy of Scripture comes from someone's own interpretation."

25 WHY SHOULD I READ THE BIBLE?

The Bible is God's way of talking to us. You would never get to know a friend very well if you always did all of the talking in the friendship and never let them say anything. The same is true with God. If you talk to God by praying, but never listen to Him by reading what He has to say, you won't get much closer to Him.

The Bible says that everything we ever needed to know about God was revealed in Jesus Christ (Hebrews 1:1-3), but since Jesus isn't walking right here with us on earth now, we have to rely on the book that's about Him – The Bible. Everything in the BIble is about Jesus.

There are rules we should follow (and these show us that we can't be perfect but need Jesus – Galatians 3:24), history to learn (and the people and events all lead up to Jesus coming), stories about Jesus himself, and letters to churches that help us all to better understand who Jesus is and why He came.

The Bible is good for teaching us, telling us what we're doing wrong, telling us what to change, and what we should start doing (2 Timothy 3:16). We should read it everyday to see what God wants us to know and so we can grow closer to Him.

Do you know 2 Peter 1:20 yet?

"knowing this first of all, that no prophecy of Scripture comes from someone's own interpretation."

26 WHO AM I?

Did you know that even before He ever created the world, God had a plan just for you (Ephesians 1:4)? He knew you and loved you before He even created you. You have a unique identity that's given to you by God. Who are you supposed to be? Who are you?

The Bible tells us a lot of things about who we are and who God expects us to be. It tells us about being made in God's image, about having a purpose, about needing God's forgiveness, and about how we all represent God as His children. We'll be looking into each of those things this week.

Start thinking right now about who you think God created you to be. What plans do you think He has for you? What will you become? How will you serve Him now and as you get older? As you read the Bible verses we cover this week, keep coming back to those questions to see if any of your answers have changed.

Ready for a new verse to memorize?
Here it is:Ephesians 2:10

"For we are his workmanship,
created in Christ Jesus for good
works, which God prepared
beforehand, that we should walk in
them."

27 I AM CREATED IN GOD'S IMAGE

God created man and woman in His own image and likeness (Genesis 1:27). Ok, but, what does that mean exactly? What does it mean to be in someone's image?

Have you ever been told that you look just like your mom or dad? Maybe someone has commented that you look a lot like an aunt or uncle or grandmother or grandfather. The fact that you look like them is because you're related, you come from the same family. You could say that you were made in the image of your parents because you bear their likeness. Get it yet?

So, we can't see God. He's invisible (1 Timothy 1:17). How can we bear someone's image if they can't be seen? The Bible says that God is spirit. Animals and plants are not spirit, rocks and dirt are not spirit. But you and I, humans, are spiritual beings. It means we can think and we can create things, we can talk and write and we can discover new things. We can worship God and be in a relationship with Him. No other thing on this earth can do that but us.

You were created to be close to God. He wants that from each one of us and it's why He created people in His image. Think today about some ways in which you're different from other created things because you're a human who is created in the likeness of God.

Keep memorizing Ephesians 2:10

"For we are his workmanship, created in Christ Jesus for good works, which God prepared beforehand, that we should walk in them."

28 I HAVE A PURPOSE

Before He ever created you- before He ever created anything – God had a purpose in mind for you. He knew what He wanted you to do and He made you perfect for that special job. Are you really good at something? God gave you that gift so you could do something for His purpose.

Everything about who you are, what you like, what you're good at, what you're not good at, these are all things that God put together into a person to make you. And He planned all that out before He even made the world! You're special in the eyes of God. No one else is you and no one else is meant to be. No one else can do exactly what God wants you to do.

It's not always easy to know what our purpose is, but if we'll pray, read the Bible to hear from God, and obey Him, we'll usually find whatever the next step is to become who we're created to be. Who do you think God made you to be? What's your purpose?

Keep working on Ephesians 2:10

"For we are his workmanship, created in Christ Jesus for good works, which God prepared beforehand, that we should walk in them."

29 I NEED GOD'S FORGIVENESS

Even though we've all been created in the image of God, just like Adam and Eve, this has been ruined some by sin. When Adam and Eve chose to sin, they made their perfect relationship with God not-so-perfect anymore. Now, every person that's come ever since them has needed God's forgiveness of their sin (through Jesus) just to have a relationship with Him.

You may not think you've done anything bad enough to need God's forgiveness, but the Bible is clear that all of us have sinned and don't meet up to God's requirement of perfection (Romans 3:23). It's also pretty clear that we can be forgiven if we ask (1 John 1:9). We just have to confess (admit that we've done wrong) and ask for His forgiveness, and He'll give it! All followers of Jesus Christ can be forgiven.

What have you done today that you know is wrong? Think about some things and talk to God. Admit to Him that you've done those things and even some others you might not realize and ask for His forgiveness.

Today's memory verse is 1 John 1:9

"If we confess our sins, he is faithful and just to forgive us our sins, and to cleanse us from all unrighteousness."

30 I REPRESENT GOD

Being made in God's image means that we represent who He is. But being His followers also means that we represent Him in a much bigger way. We represent *who* God is and *how* God is. Those who don't follow Him should see these things about Him through our example.

For instance, God is loving, so we should all be loving. We shouldn't be bullying anyone or making fun of them. We should be caring for them and showing them God's love. God is good, not evil, so we shouldn't be planning evil. We shouldn't love what's evil (Romans 12:9), but what's good.

When people see those of us who follow Jesus, they're seeing an example of what His people are supposed to be like. We've always got to be showing the right example. The Bible says when we do good works people will see them and give glory to God because of them (Matthew 5:16). Are you showing people the right things about God?

1 John 1:9 *"If we confess our sins, he is faithful and just to forgive us our sins, and to cleanse us from all unrighteousness."*

ABOUT THE AUTHOR

Matt Cochran's passion is seeing people's lives transformed by a relationship with Jesus Christ. At Christ Fellowship of Tampa, Matt helps kids from kindergarten through 5th grade in their spiritual journey as the children's ministry director.

Having served in the Marine Corps in locations all over the world, Matt easily connects with people. He holds a Bachelor's Degree in Christian Studies and a Master's Degree in Discipleship Ministries. Matt has been married to the love of his life, Rose, for ten years. They have two sons, Colin and Hank, as well as a daughter, Amelie Grace.

Read Matt's thoughts and philosophy on the topic of children's ministry at his blog, #kidmin, by visiting www.kidmin.matthewjcochran.com.

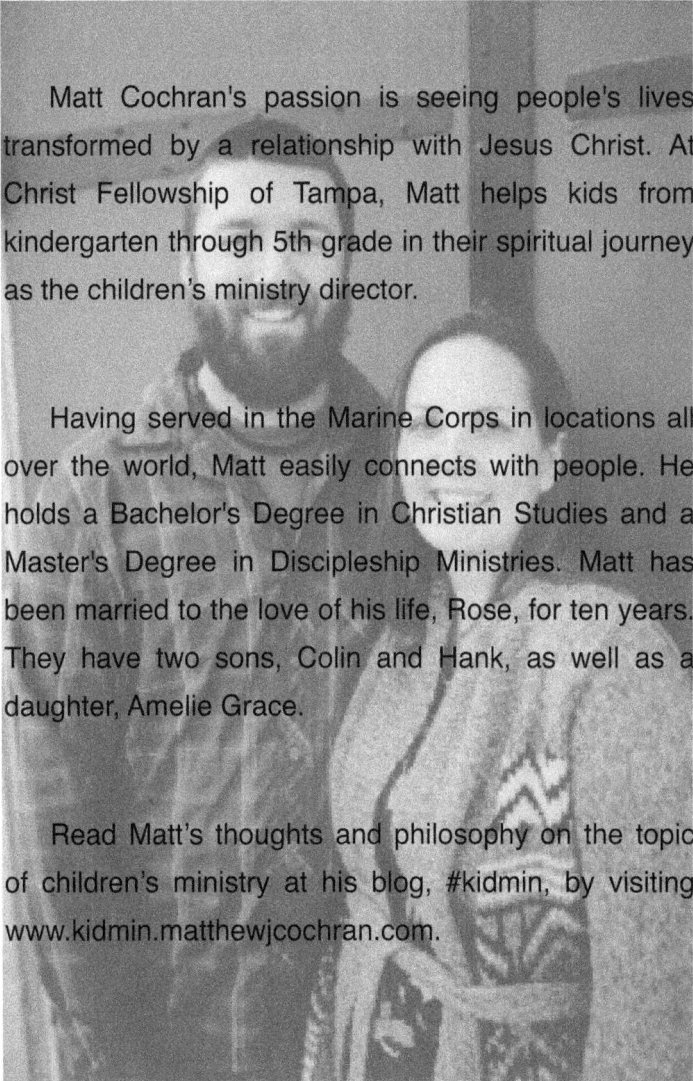

www.ingramcontent.com/pod-product-compliance
Lightning Source LLC
Chambersburg PA
CBHW071930020426
42331CB00010B/2804